JUL 0 3 2017

Country

Aaron Carr

LET'S READ
AV²
BY WEIGL™
ADDED VALUE • AUDIO VISUAL

Go to **www.av2books.com,** and enter this book's unique code.

BOOK CODE

D676545

AV² by Weigl brings you media enhanced books that support active learning.

AV² provides enriched content that supplements and complements this book. Weigl's AV² books strive to create inspired learning and engage young minds in a total learning experience.

Your AV² Media Enhanced books come alive with...

Audio
Listen to sections of the book read aloud.

Video
Watch informative video clips.

Embedded Weblinks
Gain additional information for research.

Try This!
Complete activities and hands-on experiments.

Key Words
Study vocabulary, and complete a matching word activity.

Quizzes
Test your knowledge.

Slide Show
View images and captions, and prepare a presentation.

... and much, much more!

Published by AV² by Weigl
350 5th Avenue, 59th Floor
New York, NY 10118
Website: www.av2books.com

Library of Congress Cataloging-in-Publication Data

Carr, Aaron.
  Country / Aaron Carr.
     pages cm. -- (I love music)
  Includes bibliographical references and index.
  ISBN 978-1-4896-3577-8 (hard cover : alk. paper) -- ISBN 978-1-4896-3578-5 (soft cover : alk. paper) --
  ISBN 978-1-4896-3579-2 (single user ebook) -- ISBN 978-1-4896-3580-8 (multi-user ebook)
  1. Country music--History and criticism--Juvenile literature. I. Title.
  ML3524.C32 2015
  781.64209--dc23

                              2015002869

Printed in the United States of America in Brainerd, Minnesota
1 2 3 4 5 6 7 8 9 0 19 18 17 16 15

072015
170415

Project Coordinator: Jared Siemens
Designer: Mandy Christiansen

The publisher acknowledges Alamy, Getty Images, and iStock as the primary image suppliers for this title.

Country

CONTENTS

I love music. Country is my favorite kind of music.

Country music
began in the
United States in
the early 1900s.

5

Country music came from Great Britain. Settlers brought this music to North America.

6

The first country songs were made in the southern United States.

Some of the first country singers were cowboys.

Most early country music was played on the fiddle.

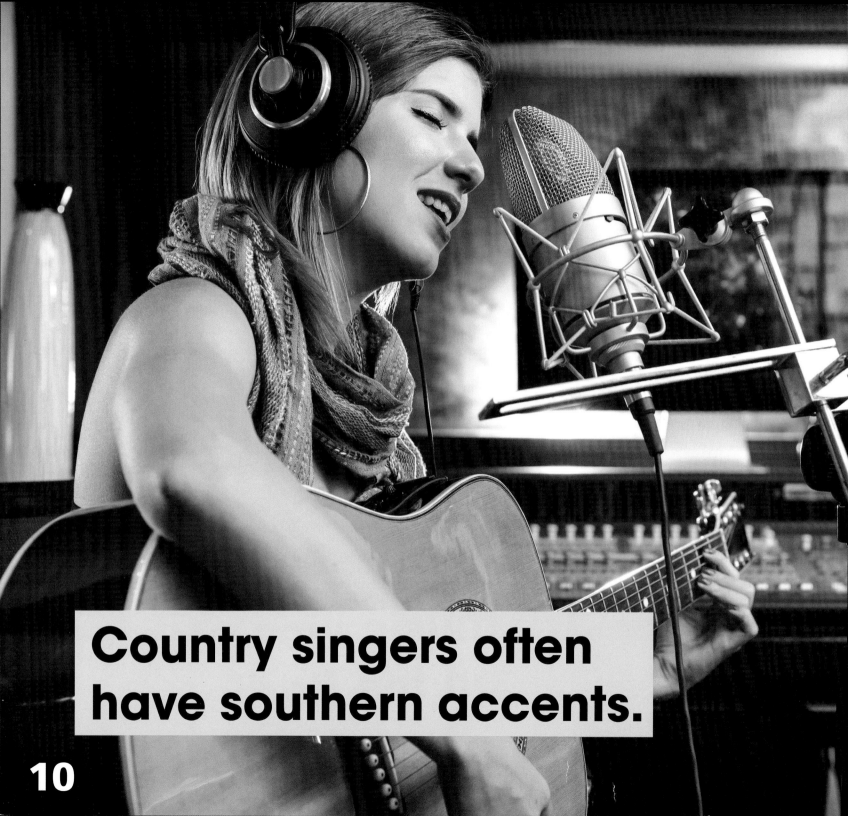

Country singers often have southern accents.

Many country
singers are known
for their twang.

11

Country songs tell stories about everyday life.

Many country songs tell love stories.

Guitars are the most important instruments in country music today.

Some country musicians play the steel guitar.

15

I like to play country music with my friends. Each person plays a different instrument.

Playing in a band teaches us how to work together.

Nashville, Tennessee, is known as the home of country music. Many country artists live and make music there.

Country musicians tour the world to play music for their fans.

19

I love country music. Playing music helps me learn new things.

COUNTRY FACTS

These pages provide detailed information that expands on the interesting facts found in the book. They are intended to be used by adults as a learning support to help young readers round out their knowledge of each musical genre featured in the *I Love Music* series.

Pages 4–5

I love music. Country is my favorite kind of music.

Country music began in the United States in the early 1900s.

I love music. Country is my favorite kind of music. Music is the name given to sounds made with voices or musical instruments and put together in a way that conveys emotion. People use music to express themselves. Country is one of the most widely played forms of music in the United States. It is most often concerned with family, conservative values, rural life, and cowboy culture. Cowboys are rugged, horse-riding individuals of western America who work with cattle.

Pages 6–7

Country music came from Great Britain. Settlers brought this music to North America.

The first country songs were made in the southern United States.

Country music came from Great Britain. Country music grew out of the folk songs early settlers brought to the American South from England, Scotland, and Ireland. These settlers used music to help keep the traditions of their old homes alive in their new country. They lived in small communities and worked hard to survive. The first country music recordings were made in the early 1920s. Before the 1940s, country music was often referred to as country and western music.

Pages 8–9

Some of the first country singers were cowboys.

Most early country music was played on the fiddle.

Some of the first country singers were cowboys. Cowboy actors such as Gene Autry helped make the cowboy image synonymous with country music. Autry was a multi-talented actor-singer who starred as a cowboy in a variety of popular western movies in the early to mid-1900s. His popularity helped launch his music career, where he went on to record "Tumbling Tumbleweeds." The fiddle's compact, affordable nature helped make it the main instrument of early country music.

Pages 10–11

Country singers often have southern accents.

Many country singers are known for their twang.

Country singers often have southern accents. With country music's rural origins, it is not surprising that country singers have a vocal style that reflects these roots. Country singers tend to stress the accents of their speaking voices in their singing voices. The twang in some country vocals comes from the amount of nasal resonance in a singer's voice. This occurs when air made by vocal sounds is allowed to pass through and vibrate in the nasal cavity.

Country songs often tell stories about everyday life. From its earliest beginnings to today, country music has always placed a high importance on storytelling. The lyrical focus of the earliest country songs included characters with simple lives and strong work ethics. Some of the most prominent themes in country lyrics today are love, heartbreak, and a celebration of rural American culture.

Guitars are the most important instrument in country music today. Although traditional country music was played on fiddles, acoustic and electric guitars eventually came to define modern country style. Other instruments used in country include the banjo, bass, washboard, dobro, mandolin, and harmonica. Today, most country bands have guitars, basses, and drums. Drums did not become common in country music until the 1960s.

I like to play country music with my friends. Playing music with others helps teach children cooperation, teamwork, and how to achieve goals. Children who regularly play music tend to have more confidence and get along better with others. Some students learn better in groups because they do not feel the pressure of having to learn on their own.

Nashville, Tennessee, is known as the home of country music. Nashville is home of the *Grand Ole Opry*, whose radio broadcasts helped spread country music to the rest of the nation and established the city as the center of country music. The Country Music Hall of Fame and Museum is also located in Nashville. Today, country artists such as Carrie Underwood and Blake Shelton tour the globe playing shows in arenas, stadiums, and music festivals.

I love country music. Playing music helps me learn new things. Recent studies suggest that learning and practicing music can be beneficial to a child's ability to learn. Among these benefits are improved motor skills and dexterity, increased test scores, and even raised Intelligence Quotient, or IQ, scores. Learning music at an early age has also been shown to aid in language development, and to improve reading and listening skills.

KEY WORDS

Research has shown that as much as 65 percent of all written material published in English is made up of 300 words. These 300 words cannot be taught using pictures or learned by sounding them out. They must be recognized by sight. This book contains 54 common sight words to help young readers improve their reading fluency and comprehension. This book also teaches young readers several important content words. These words are paired with pictures to aid in learning and improve understanding.

Page	Sight Words First Appearance	Page	Content Words First Appearance
4	I, is, kind, my, of	4	country, music
5	began, in, states, the	5	United States
6	came, from, this, to	6	Great Britain, North America, settlers
7	first, made, songs, were	8	singers, cowboys
8	some	9	fiddle
9	most, on, was	10	accents
10	have, often	11	twang
11	are, for, known, many, their	12	stories
12	about, life, tell	14	guitars, instruments
14	important	15	steel guitar
15	play	16	friends
16	a, different, each, like, with	17	band
17	how, together, us, work	18	Nashville, Tennessee
18	and, as, home, live, make, there	19	fans
19	world		
21	helps, learn, me, new, things		

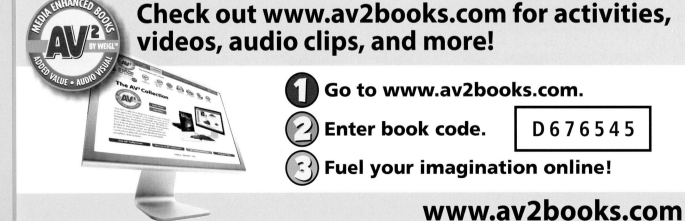